PERSPECTIVES IN A PANDEMIC

T0326976

PERSPECTIVES IN A PANDEMIC

Kevin M. Cahill, M.D.

Refuge Press, New York, 2020

Copyright©2020
The Center for International Humanitarian
Cooperation
Fordham University IHA Book Series
All rights reserved.
No part of this book may be reproduced
or utilized in any form or by any means,
electronic or mechanical, including
photocopying and recording, or by any
information storage and retrieval system
without permission in writing from the
publishers.

ISBN #13: 978-0-8232-9498-5
All royalties from this book go to the
training of humanitarian workers.

Cover design: Mauro Sarri
Cover Image courtesy of NASA

The logo of the CIHC, used as a printer's
device to separate each section,
symbolizes the unity of healing hands in
relief work with the doves for peace.

Printed in the United States of America.

For the Marias Aramanda

Table of Contents

Introduction

Within a few months after a new coronavirus (COVID-19) was first detected in December 2019 in Wuhan, China, local outbreaks, usually attributed to recent travelers, were reported in many parts of the world. In the United States of America the epicenter soon became New York City. Hospitals were overwhelmed with critically ill patients, many requiring life support with ventilators and respirators. Healthcare providers, after facing shortages of protective gear, confused instructions from federal and local authorities, faulty testing materials, and no approved drug therapy or vaccine available, reverted to ancient—but effective—public health measures such as isolation and quarantine, a focus on facial masks, and handwashing.

My own medical facility, Lenox Hill Hospital in New York, converted to an almost fully COVID-19 institution; all elective medical and surgical procedures were cancelled and patient rooms were converted into intensive care units. Between mid-March and early June 2020, Lenox Hill Hospital admitted 1,415 COVID-19 patients, with many deaths particularly in the elderly population.

My personal physicians were pointing

out that age and some underlying medical problems made my presence in the hospital dangerous, and counterproductive. Another sick or dying doctor would be an unnecessary burden on an already fragile system. Since my career in tropical medicine dealing with the complexities of international humanitarian crises, and in training medical students and relief workers had exposed me to the problems of earlier epidemics, I began a weekly letter of support to our alumni and colleagues for the critical first phase of three months. The reports were well received, and are collected in this brief book as a record of our ongoing efforts. In a pandemic, the "frontline" is not defined by any single hospital but rather in multiple roles, in many places, all around the world. The Dedication reflects the generosity of Marias Aramanda, mother and daughter. They helped in the editing and revising on the last six texts in the International Humanitarian Affairs Book Series, making the process a joyous one.

It is tempting to indulge in the dangerous deceit that we are experiencing unprecedented suffering during the current COVID-19 pandemic. There are many examples in the history of medicine of how society survived previous major health crises, often after great loss of life, changes in government and management, and the folly of daily desperate announcements of quick solutions to complex, seemingly intractable problems. But time and human ingenuity ultimately prevailed, and new dawns rose with eternal hope. There is an obvious difference between a global pandemic and regional epidemics, but lessons learned in the former situations can be useful in the present.

Few have been privileged to direct such relief efforts. My professional career has allowed me to work in 65 countries, mostly after natural disasters or armed conflicts, trying to provide assistance to hundreds of thousands of displaced people. I would be an obstacle—at this point in my life—rather than a help in a frontline hospital setting. But having taught tropical medicine to over 4,000 students, and established multi-disciplinary programs for over 3,000 humanitarian relief workers from over 140 nations, I continue to serve. Many alumni see me as their Professor, and I receive daily telephone and electronic messages from around the world seeking advice. The contributions I can make at this moment in history have been to offer reflective essays on lessons learned beginning with Somalia after the Sahel drought in the mid-1970s.

Somalia

I first went to Somalia in the early 1960s, studying the diseases of a neglected land by following nomads as they crisscrossed the barren desert and harsh brush lands seeking water and food for their camel herds. Eventually I walked the length of the country, publishing my research findings in several books and numerous scientific papers. I continued to go to Somalia for thirtyfive consecutive years, coming to know their people as few Westerners had, and they came to know me as one who was with them in troubled times.

After the Sahel Drought in 1974 drove many thousand hungry and starving displaced persons to the Somali borders, I was asked to direct the nation's refugee response. Many disciplines are involved in creating a nation's management of an emerging disaster. As someone with a medical and public health background I have watched colleagues presume, in press conferences and publications, that they should be in the lead, that only they have the answers. But this does not reflect reality.

Only an official government has the legitimacy to be the final arbiter, whether that be under military rule, as in Somalia at that time, or some fashion of democracy, as favored in the West. Certainly the middle of an epidemic is not the time to resolve questions of political credibility. Only a recognized government can secure international aid; donors must be cautious in imposing their philosophical beliefs as "strings" on assistance. Only governments can deal with the unstable tensions that come with the movements of large populations from distant lands, with different languages, cultures, clan structures, and religious beliefs. The health director must participate, but not confuse or add to confusion, by intruding publicly in debates on security, camp sites, distribution of essential shelter, food and water. Ideally this can be done under United Nations aegis, but political realities will often determine where global attention is focused. In the Somali-Sahel catastrophe there was a far greater awareness of the needs of boat people fleeing Vietnam, reflecting America's obsession with a lost war, rather than the more extreme problems faced by other suffering populations.

My task was to establish, as rapidly as possible, camps that would serve the healthy, and try to triage the sick and dying. There were few doctors and nurses, and large numbers of patients with malaria, overt tuberculosis, cholera, dysentery, upper respiratory infection and festering wounds. New arrivals had to be screened by a cadre of volunteers, poorly trained by even the most basic standards of public health.

For a period I deployed a color coded health system where a local dresser was given a tin can with ten different colored pills. He/she gave a red pill to someone coughing up blood on the presumption it could well be tuberculosis. If it was cancer there was nothing we could offer anyway. Cholera patients usually died because we had no ability to replenish the large volume of intravenous fluid necessary to save their lives. The dead had to be buried, and, somehow, children had to be protected and provided with a semblance of school under a tree. Still, while some functions could—or should—progress without government assistance, an attempt to force change in the political-cultural structure of a nation in the middle of an epidemic is an arrogant, futile, and destructive activity.

If done with the dignity and respect that the healing arts have earned by thousands of years of professional service to all, especially vulnerable populations, then a system can be created to map a path out of chaos.

While America's current "top scientist" Dr. Anthony Fauci, has had a very impressive career directing a federal Institute at the NIH, those skills may not be adequate for the complex issues of an epidemic/pandemic. The skills necessary to be an administrator, or a laboratory scientist, or in supervising the teams that develop new drugs and vaccine strains, may be far removed from the experience required in managing large scale disaster relief programs. Fortunately, Dr. Fauci can draw on his Jesuit educational background, with its focus on the broad liberal arts, on anthropology classes, studies in classical literature and philosophy. Certainly, in my work in epidemics, these disciplines were more helpful than the details of biochemistry. In fact, there were little in the medical school curriculum of that era that helped guide me in establishing refugee camps. Dr. Fauci's professional demeanor, his overt humility, and his desire to assist in the multi-dimensional catastrophe is a source of great pride to his fellow physicians.

We are entering a new world where action may not be an adequate measure when imaginative and creative thoughts and ideas are needed. I wish I had a more definitive advice to offer but I don't.

No one has captured better than Albert Camus, in his 1947 novel, The Plague, the unique exile an epidemic imposes:

The plague swallowed up everything and everyone. No longer were there individual destinies, only a collective destiny, made of plague and the emotions shared by all. Strongest of these emotions was the sense of exile and of deprivation, with all the cross currents of revolt and fears set up by these.

And the book concludes:

...that Dr. Rieux resolved to compile this chronicle, so that he should not be one of those who hold their peace but should bear witness in favor of those plague stricken people; so that some memorial of the injustice and outrage done them might endure; and to state quite simply what we learn in time of pestilence: that there are more things to admire in men than to despise.

Nicaragua

Shortly before midnight on December 23, 1972, an earthquake destroyed the capital city of Nicaragua. Less than an hour later I was asked by their government to direct the public health response; the American Embassy facilitated arrangements. I arrived by military flight shortly before dawn. The city was ablaze, with the earth still shaking from numerous aftershocks. One of the more bizarre aspects of my passage through the airport was meeting Howard Hughes, the reclusive billionaire who had been living in a hotel in Managua. The American ambassador was clearly more committed to escorting his guest safely out of the country than in greeting the new American health envoy.

The immediate disaster relief principles were obvious, search for the wounded and remove them, and everyone, to the periphery where triage, treatment centers and temporary shelter could be established. There were few medical supplies, and no coordination of health workers except for the National Guard under the control of President Anastasio Somoza. I was invited to live in a tent with the President and used that as my headquarters for the next six weeks.

After the Nicaragua earthquake, there was, as in all public health crises, a gradual imposition of order over chaos. Security in Nicaragua was enforced by the National Guard. Looting in the streets was curtailed, roads cleared, and buses & trucks could move populations to safe sites outside the earthquake zone, allowing families to reunite and begin life anew.

The American government response was immediate, practical and, initially, deeply appreciated. The United States deployed a fully equipped portable one-hundred-bed field hospital complete with doctors, nurses, trauma surgeons, and anesthesiologists. There were no other functioning hospitals in Nicaragua of this caliber, and it provided superb care in the critical first few weeks after the earthquake. The cultural differences between a military facility and the customs of Nicaragua, however, led to growing tensions.

In most Nicaraguan hospitals families gathered around the sick bed trying to comfort the patient with home-cooked meals, a favorite blanket, sometimes a smuggled-in pet. The American military insisted on orderliness, and would eject the families. Also, and understandably, Nicaraguan medical personnel wanted access to the American military facility, and resented their exclusion in their own country. The United States-Nicaragua relationship has been a tortured one for well over a century, with frequent armed intervention by the all-powerful nation from the north. Further, as the situation stabilized there were, almost inevitably, social contacts between the American military staff and local women that led to rumors and allegations of illicit activity. I became convinced that the "honeymoon" period of gratitude was fading fast after the first six weeks.

The international response to the earthquake was also generous and rapid. Massive donations began to arrive at the airport. Because I lived with President Somoza—and worked daily with the Core Coordinating Committee—I saw firsthand how these donations were stored in new warehouses, and distributed by cronies of the ruling family. Corruption was an obvious problem as many donations were soon available for sale all around Managua. There was no official criticism from the United States government for fear of further destabilizing President Somoza's control of a fragile country.

In a *Congressional Report*, I praised the rapid U.S. response, the professional triage, surgical and medical care provided, but noted the negatives due to a failed military-civil interaction. Prior to this period, I had been in close contact with Nicaraguan clergy who were developing the nascent Sandinista movement that would eventually overthrow the Somoza regime. To the credit of both parties neither ever asked me about the other; medicine, if practiced with dignity, respect and adhering to the ancient Hippocratic principles of confidentiality, can be a bridge crossing the most hostile barriers. These lessons remain valid today in the current pandemic, as the temptation to blame different levels of government, for obvious failures in preparedness is the frequent recourse of politicians. Far better to develop a functioning, productive health system that can resolve problems and prevent unnecessary deaths.

The lessons learned during that period are relevant to our response to the current pandemic. They are also part of the cement that bind the CIHC/IIHA family together. These are shared memories where I can identify with your current experiences, and, hopefully, you with mine. They are tales that keep the past alive and provide a needed perspective lest we forget the long history of previous plagues, and of ultimate recovery. Recalling lessons also allows this Professor to maintain the ancient obligation of academia to stay in contact with those he trained, and to support their own efforts in dealing with the challenges of a new generation. You have new tools to better stay in touch with one another while I mostly rely on the old fashioned method of analyzing recollections in writing.

Brendan—and his team—have been able to continue our educational courses using the IT techniques of distant learning, skills that seem to elude me. We have, however, had to cancel the upcoming IDHA course because the 35 candidates from 22 countries around the world made it almost impossible to maintain the personal interaction between teacher and student that has characterized our unique programs with over 3,000 alumni from 140 nations. Many international, governmental and NGO agencies view the IDHA as the "gold standard in humanitarian training", and we should change the format only after careful considerations.

South Sudan

Many years ago I experienced a prolonged period of solitude while working in a U.S. Navy Research Unit in South Sudan. Shortly after I arrived in a conflict zone in Malakal, 500 miles beyond Khartoum, all missionaries were declared *persona non grata* and forced to leave the country. Since they were almost the only Westerners in the area, and were the primary providers of healthcare, I found myself without personal or professional contacts. I felt alone, but not lonely, and realized that this was time for reflections, time to consider that imaginative ideas were often more important than repetitive actions, and that a well conceived plan was an essential foundation for long lasting progress.

It was a formative, probably life-changing experience. The solitude forced me to choose new directions, to make decisions not influenced by the transient concerns of the moment, and to build a foundation that could simultaneously sustain multiple endeavors. One learned the futility of merely bemoaning a fate imposed, not chosen, and to somehow create new programs out of adversity.

My perception and perspective of the world around me changed. Details of our research project were grounded in science, but I recognized there was an essential role for love and trust and sharing if I was to accomplish my goals in a crisis situation. There were few guidelines available but inner strengths emerged in that period in South Sudan, and have served me well over the decades.

We are currently stalled in the highly infectious—often lethal—COVID-19 outbreak, with political rumors, or blame all about. I once again send a message to our "family" of humanitarian workers and physicians who I have tried to help prepare for these challenges. None of us could have predicted the extent of the global dysfunction but the history of previous plagues provides hope rather than despair.

I was once asked to name the most memorable country in which I had worked. I chose South Sudan for reasons that are perhaps relevant to the climate we endure during the present pandemic. I spent four months in Malakal, where the various local tribes were intent on eliminating each other, and the process was facilitated by perverse interventions from the national government in Khartoum. The expulsion of the missionaries was an effective death threat to those ill with treatable diseases, to the wounded, and to the local and public health programs. I found myself as one of a handful of clinicians in a vast area, and that allowed me to transcend the limited goals of my Navy research assignment.

A primary lesson in disaster relief work is that one must stay healthy—not only to survive but to be able to serve others. This is not a selfish exercise but a recognition of our own frailty in the midst of epidemic infections. Adequate rest, a decent diet and personal exercise are important components of the humanitarian's daily regime. I usually begin my training program for new candidates in this noble field by stating, simply but directly, that you will do no good for anyone if you fall ill.

My routine in South Sudan was to arise early, have a modest breakfast of fruit and bread, do an indoor exercise (because there were usually large snakes around the small house) and prepare a schedule for the day. One could not always adhere to the program but it was well to delineate goals. I would also suggest that it is important to keep a diary; it allows one to assess recent activities, and years later to be reminded of the bygone challenges one unexpectedly faces in life.

The research activities—the formal reason the U.S. Navy had assigned me to the area—was to collect specimens in a project studying a specific parasitic disease, Leishmaniasis. Since my predecessors had been PhD scientists, the focus had been on species identification and animal vectors; but as a medical doctor I was more interested in the clinical signs, symptoms and response to therapy. My major contribution was to demonstrate that the Leishmania organism could give a radically different presentation in a well-nourished Westerner than in the local population. Factors, including basic nutrition and concurrent anti-malarial drugs had not been considered.

The research specimens were sent to our main laboratory in Cairo, Egypt. Here the packages met a fate that the world is dealing with in the current pandemic—the intrusion of super power politics in a humanitarian operation. Packages—even scientific specimens—could not be sent from Egypt to the WHO reference lab in Israel; they had to be first sent to Geneva, Switzerland before repackaging and transfer to Tel Aviv. This caused unreasonable delays, but no one dared comment on this ridiculous folly.

The remainder of my day in Malakal was devoted to medical and public health projects. I shall cite but one example of an adaptation to reality on the ground. An indigenous healer had served the community for many years—using ashes, chicken bones and incantations—to divine out evil forces. I had a modest supply of modern Western drugs and equipment, and a confidence in my technical skills in healing. But rather than have a confrontation—since I realized that he would stay long after my four month tour in the area ended—I proposed we work together. He had the essential community outreach, and the trust of the tribal leader. There was simply no reason to waste precious time emphasizing the contrasts in our approaches to clinical problems, and so we cooperated in helping the sick. The system worked well, and I departed on schedule strongly suspecting the healer would continue to serve, especially in the absence of the missionary health clinics.

Once again I close this letter by noting how proud we are of your work, and sending along the prayers of your teachers and colleagues that you stay safe and well.

Foundations

This series of reflections suggest that there is a relevance to what many of you now face in dealing with the current COVID-19 pandemic. This 'Perspective' will consider some predictable dangers—both philosophic and personal—that, if unchecked—can both harm us, and our humanitarian assistance efforts.

Philosophic

The existential principles of humanitarian relief are our beliefs in neutrality, impartiality, and respect for human beings wounded in wars, after disasters, or caught as innocent civilians in the crossfires of conflict. For many centuries these principles were unwritten, until codified in the Geneva Conventions and international law. These are the guidelines that, when followed, can allow peace to be gradually restored; such, obviously, is not always the case.

The principle of "impartiality" has been respected, ideally, by the victors for those vanquished. The wounded need care, and societies need to heal. Neutrality and impartiality must be re-emphasized, again and again, in every generation.

These philosophical bases are usually accepted, even between recent enemies, if presented in a Socratic fashion in which probing but respectful questions can lead towards a re-evaluation of previously rigid positions. The potential of dialogue cannot be overemphasized.

Even among humanitarian workers there may well be radically different approaches suggested. A military person, for example, might try to impose a solution that is counter to those trained in psychiatry and the healing arts. Both must learn to understand the ethos of the other.

There was a time—and a very good time it was—when I could have shared these experiences with you in the field. Now my best contribution is to be available to those we have trained, to see if lessons from earlier crises can help you in dealing with the current pandemic. On an average day I talk to colleagues in ten to fifteen countries, where our alumni are coping with the unknown.

Personal

In conflict or post-conflict zones, thousands of internally displaced victims flee to refugee camps, but long-term hatreds are not stopped by a gate. The humanitarian relief worker must provide not only food and shelter, but be part of the negotiations towards reestablishing security and communal stability. These are expected, recurrent problems.

The confusion of, and competition between, armed forces is a growing danger in most war zones with fringe elements often outnumbering national forces. Within the past month a plane delivering aid, in a remote area of Somalia I once knew well, was shot down as it tried to land. On the ground were contingents from the Somali *Shabab*, the African Union, Ethiopian forces and troops from Kenya. From the sky, U.S. drones sent missiles, with innocent civilians killed as "collateral damage".

Many of you who have worked in similar troubled areas may recall the fear at roadblocks, where, too often, a teenager with an AK-47—often incoherent on *khat*— thrusts his weapon through an open window and demands papers (or any valuables).

My car was once stopped fourteen times on the ten hour ride from Djibouti to Hargeisa in Northern Somalia. I can still see the faces of those who might, by accident or intent, have killed us—or allowed us to proceed after some cigarettes and banter were exchanged. We have incorporated advice in our training programs for staying safe in such situations: remain calm, do not argue, keep both hands visible on the steering wheel, and a light on the inside roof of the car or truck, and let a local guide try to provide whatever official papers may be helpful.

Some of the most memorable letters in our Institute's files are from alumni who remembered these lessons when they were held hostage; notes of gratitude that they were still alive because they followed the IDHA course recommendations. Training is imperative if problems are predictable.

In the chaos that often follows natural disasters there is often civil unrest, with looting and the settling of old grudges. These are times when the prudent relief worker stays put in the refugee compound so that they can serve when calm is re-established. These are normal, daily challenges in what we know can be the very abnormal profession of humanitarian assistance.

Once a camp is established foreseeable problems almost always emerge. There is often difficulty assuring adequate supplies of food, water and shelter, and this is sometimes further compounded by supply theft, incompetence, corruption, and a lack of coordination with other agencies. These problems can also be magnified by outside politicians who seek publicity in disasters, and by pressure from donor nations—not only for reports but to foster their own goals. Colin Powell, as U.S. Secretary of State, viewed humanitarian relief workers as "force-multipliers", to push a particular foreign policy agenda. This view was condemned by almost all United Nations, national, and non-governmental organizations who perceive the strength of their positions as grounded in neutrality and impartiality.

If not handled properly these challenges can rapidly, and completely, destroy the integrity of our work. We can become complicit by a silent acquiescence with such approaches. But one also learns that contentious arguments are usually destructive, and that the best way forward is to enunciate the principles that have been the foundation of humanitarian relief for thousands of years, and then move ahead calmly, and with confidence.

Finally, I again note that your own physical and mental health are vitally important. Maintaining an adequate diet and periods of rest are essential; you will do no good for anyone if you fall ill and have to be evacuated. I also found that keeping a diary allowed me to record scenes that too easily can be overlooked—sunrises, sunsets, the smile of a child. These provide a balance to sordid and sad images, and help avoid depression. You must find your own way to a steady path, but a diary, artwork, or a letter to be saved for a loved one, might be a healthy part of your plan.

The wise humanitarian learns that to persevere is a goal in itself. As Samuel Beckett once said of humanity's struggle in difficult times: "I'll go on". Serving those who are suffering and in need of our assistance—trudging ahead—is our privileged role. This should result in a cumulative reward, providing we avoid the personal problems that can prevent us carrying on in humanitarian work.

You can also stay in touch with Larry, Brendan, your tutors and classmates to seek counsel, based on a companionship forged in our unique field. Stay safe and warmest regards.

An Easter Offering

As a sequel to my initial reflections on lessons learned in large scale epidemics and disaster relief work in many parts of the world, I here offer some thoughts on the basic values that guide our efforts in such situation. Now the CIHC/IIHA family is on the frontlines in hospitals and public health services struggling against the COVID-19 pandemic while I am under quarantine in isolation thinking proudly of your work and hopeful that you remain safe as well.

Various virtues help us survive during difficult times.

There is no substitute for steady hard work demanded during an epidemic. There are long, exhausting days of triage, and in trying to assist the very ill to recovery.

One must remain calm amidst confusion and be decisive in making critical choices, especially when there appear too few alternatives.

There is a solidarity that develops between those privileged to provide help and the beneficiaries.

The leaders must instill a sense of compassion as well as competency.

All our tasks must be done with humility, and a modesty that recognizes the multi-disciplinary contribution of a team approach.

The overall program should be, whenever possible, coordinated, but under constant review to avoid rigidity and promote adaptability, prudence, honesty and transparency concerning data, goals and failures.

With tenacity and vision, and, once again, steady hard work, the history of medicine gives us confidence that we shall prevail.

We must express our gratitude for this opportunity to participate in a great crisis, and to record our services in a diary for posterity.

A final obligation is to distill the current approaches into a body of wisdom that can be taught to a new generation of humanitarians.

God speed.

Family

Previous pieces in this series have explored personal lessons learned in earlier epidemics, in Somalia, Nicaragua, and the South Sudan, and in the shared values and virtues that sustain us in such situations. This message will focus on one element common to those we have trained—through our courses and publications—to be caring, compassionate and professional. This is the cement that binds us together and offers a solid foundation for our efforts; it is a type of glue that links IDHA classmates, and provides common ground for the alumni of our other programs, all trying to serve in these challenging times. Some of you are in hospitals or the military delivering frontline assistance; some of you are in senior government and NGO positions providing policy and advice to mitigate a way out of the dark night. We are part of a critical "family" of humanitarian relief workers. The goal of creating such a "family" is at the very core of our CIHC/IIHA programs and it is most gratifying to see it in your frequent reports.

There were fundamental decisions made in the early planning stages—to develop courses, symposiums, and publications that were field oriented, practical, and comprehensive. Teachers, tutors and most candidates were selected almost solely from those who had experienced the realities of work in crisis zones and refugee camps. But we also had to meet strict academic standards so that our graduates would have the legitimacy and credibility that only a university can confer in a diploma or degree. Curricula would be offered all over the world, but the form, content and individual dialogue approach would be always based on the unique philosophy that was initiated twentyfive years ago.

Since many of those details have been published in *Milestones in Humanitarian Action* and as part of the IHA Book Series available in both print and digital format, I provide them here as references. How does one build a sense of "family"? Our usual IDHA class had 35 candidates from over 20 nations with an average age of 38 years. We have now offered 54 IDHA courses in dozens of nations on every continent. They were to live together, with the tutors, for one month in a program that tried to simulate the tensions—and forced camaraderie—of a disaster relief area. The class was broken down into "syndicates" of 5-7 students who had to coalesce as a team. Part of their academic grading was based on how well they accomplished this essential effort of a "family". Some candidates helped those who had long forgotten the demands of academia, or had problems with language, or were lonely or depressed. As with most "family" efforts, the first weeks were sometimes a bit difficult but by the end of the month most classes had come together and graduated as one, proud of each other. With the follow-up help of CIHC/IIHA staff, most have stayed in contact, and enrolled in our other specialized courses such as mental health and conflicts, and many have proceeded to further graduate degrees in the field.

May these reflections find you well. Stay safe. The world needs your skill and wisdom.

Training From Reality

Transferring knowledge to a new generation is an ancient obligation in medicine; the Hippocratic Oath (in 400 BC) still taken today as physicians begin their careers, asks the following commitment:

To hold him who has taught me this art as equal to my parents and to live my life in partnership with him, and if he is in need of money to give him a share of mine, and to regard his offspring as equal to my brothers and to teach them this art—if they desire to learn it—without fee and covenant; to give a share of precepts and oral instruction and all the other learning to my sons and to the sons of him who has instructed me.

A similar requirement is true for the "family" of humanitarian workers trained by the CIHC/IIHA.

Teaching requires different and additional skills beyond those, for example, in clinical medicine, diagnosing and treating a sick patient. To be a teacher in humanitarian relief work, one must be able to extract the essential lessons of many disciplines, and be able to present these in an orderly fashion.

In times past in medicine this was accomplished by an apprentice observing at the bedside in a participatory manner. Gradually a lecture format was devised, later aided by technological advances such as visual slides and powerpoint presentations. Long before there were universities, or academic standards to be satisfied, the good teacher had to fashion his topics into an organized program, a curriculum that could be replicated and win the respect of disciples. Ultimately, it was the teacher passing on to the student their knowledge, experience and wisdom. Selecting the right persons to be teachers was critical.

In our CIHC/IIHA programs for workers in international humanitarian assistance I have always selected those "who have paid their dues", people who have worked on the frontlines after disasters or conflicts and know the realities of refugee camps. There is no substitute for this background—no credibility or legitimacy in the eyes of students—without these field experiences.

Very often, at least in medical centers, titles of Professor or Chairman may be misleading; top scientists may have made outstanding contributions based on laboratory findings but many have never seen the clinical—or societal—impacts of diseases in person.

I recall once bringing a world famous parasitologist to Somalia, only to discover he was simply not suited for the harsh scenes of a refugee camp. He quickly returned to his American laboratory and that decision was appropriate. My comments are not meant as a criticism, for each must define where they can best serve themselves as well as a world in need.

I close these reflections with a memorable image. When Andre Malraux visited a dying Charles De Gaulle, he considered his friend's legacy. He suggested that while De Gaulle had been a soldier, a politician and a writer he would be best remembered for his role as a teacher of a nation adrift. Malraux wrote that, "at one time he held the corpse of France upright, and made the world know it was still alive."

Keep your own records of this pandemic. They will help you transfer knowledge and wisdom to the next generation of relief workers. You have a rare opportunity during these unusual days to also provide an historical basis for our shared efforts to help heal a world adrift. Teaching, like prevention, is not as dramatic as treating those in urgent need of care, but it is a critical element in the still evolving definition of

our profession of international humanitarian assistance.

My best wishes to you and your families
during these difficult times.

The Other Prong

After thirty years dealing with humanitarian crises following natural disasters and conflict, I began in the early 1990s to establish formal academic programs so that our evolving knowledge of this complex discipline might be fashioned into curricula that would help train a new generation, establish best standards of good practice, and be able to provide degrees and diplomas to our candidates. That was one part of a two prong effort, and it succeeded beyond our best expectations; as noted earlier in these 'Perspectives' we now have 3,000 graduates from 140 nations, a cadre of humanitarian leaders working all around the world, and now training their own students at the local and regional level. The other prong was to publish books and Occasional Papers that could be available as a consistent source of information. There are now seventeen books and a dozen shorter papers in this International Humanitarian Affairs (IHA) Book Series; they include:

History and Hope: The International Humanitarian Reader is a compendium drawn from some of the best chapters on various aspects of humanitarian assistance that Fordham University Press has published since 2001. These books were composed with colleagues who also believed it was possible to distill our experiences from the harsh settings of crises into practical, field oriented, courses of university level quality.

The IHA Book Series began with *Preventive Diplomacy: Stopping Wars Before They Start*, a text that argued for recognition of the centrality of humanitarian action in foreign policy; they were usually peripheral afterthoughts overshadowed by other national interests. The contributors utilized the methodology of public health and the semantics of medicine in addressing the softer discipline of diplomacy. The second volume, *Tradition, Values and Humanitarian Action,* was also a philosophic book assessing what influences determine how both individuals and societies develop healthy—or destructive—policies and practices in international humanitarian assistance. Both those volumes provided solid foundations for the technical texts that followed.

The next two titles, *Emergency Relief Operations* and *Basics of Humanitarian Action* are self-explanatory. These books were primers that were needed as our academic programs developed. The chapters reflect the strong conviction that our texts (and teachers) should be deeply grounded in the difficult realities that are standard in complex emergencies. The next volume is the most personal. *To Bear Witness: A Journey of Healing and Solidarity* is a compilation of personal editorial pieces, unpublished lectures, short essays and introductions to earlier books.

The following three books provided more detailed information on specific problems. *Human Security for All: A Tribute to Sergio Vieira de Mello* was to honor the memory of a good friend who had paid the ultimate price for attempting to help those in humanitarian distress. *Technology and Humanitarian Action* evolved from my experience as Chief Medical Advisor for Counterterrorism in the New York City Police Department. Scientists associated with the U.S. Defense Advanced Research Policy Agency (DARPA) proposed imaginative technological solutions to many of the problems we faced in dealing with serious biological, chemical, and radiologic threats. As contact with these men and women deepened, it became very obvious how the intellectual and financial resources devoted to defense concerns dwarfed the attention given to the overwhelming, often intractable, problems that are the routine concerns for humanitarian workers. *Tropical Medicine: A Clinical Text* reflects my own professional background, as well as the cruel fact that in war zones, and after disasters, more people die of the treatable—and usually preventable—diseases that are the subject of this textbook. The eighth edition is a "Jubilee" version reflecting its use in medical education for over fifty years.

The next title, *The Pulse of Humanitarian Assistance*, also derives from my medical training. Taking the pulse—a basic diagnostic tool in medicine—is an ancient and trusted clinical exercise. So, too, one can measure the pulse of humanitarian action, and offer prognoses—predicting a way forward. If one is to address human suffering, and the confusion that characterizes complex humanitarian crises, then the etiologic significance of poverty, ignorance, corruption, as well as incompetence, and the all too often evil effects of religion and politics, are as valid areas to consider as the life cycles of microbes or the rhythm of the heartbeat.

Even in Chaos: Education in Times of

Emergency and *More with Less: Disasters in an Era of Diminishing Resources* were books developed during my time as Chief Advisor for Humanitarian and Public Health Issues for three Presidents of the United Nations General Assembly (PGA). The PGA is the most senior position of the United Nations, and reflects the interests of all 193 Member States.

The Open Door:Art and Foreign Policy at the Royal College of Surgeons in Ireland (RCSI) is a collection of Distinguished Lectures delivered in a Department I directed in Dublin. This annual event welcomed a Secretary General of the United Nations, a Prime Minister, four Foreign Ministers, two Nobel Laureates (in Literature and Peace), world famous actress, a renowned artist, and two physicians-philosophers to enrich the College, and also allowed the Lecturers to share in some of the ancient traditions of medicine.

An Unfinished Tapestry reviews a six year period during which I managed a large public health system in the United States of America with 80,000 employees and an annual budget of 7 billion dollars; it compares domestic programs during a fiscal crisis with the challenges of overseas disaster relief work.

A Dream for Dublin, tells the arduous—but usually joyous—creation of a Department of International Health and Tropical Medicine at the RCSI. During a 36 year tenure as Professor and Chairman, I taught over 4,000 medical students from Ireland, Europe, and many countries in Africa and Asia.

Milestones in Humanitarian Action documents the development of the Institute of Humanitarian Assistance (IIHA) at Fordham University in New York. During the last quarter century, the IIHA has offered multiple courses, including the IDHA, Mental Health in War Zones, and other specialized topics, as well as a Master's Degree and an undergraduate Major in this discipline (one of only four in the world). The last chapter is entitled *"Preventive Diplomacy"* and provides a direct link to the first book in this Series.

Labyrinths is a personal reflection that explores the influences of my childhood, education and early work in overseas crises and refugee camps.

The full Table of Contents of each book is available at *www.fordham.edu/iiha*. Seven of the texts are available in French, and others in Spanish, Italian, Portuguese, Arabic, and Japanese translations. Bernard Kouchner, the co-founder of Medicines Sans Frontieres and, later, Foreign Minister of France, wrote Forewords for several of the books. It is important to note that the contributors include the leading authorities in this field from the United Nations, national and non-governmental organizations in this field representing Doctors Without Borders (MSF), the ICRC, IFRC, International Rescue Committee, Catholic Relief Services, World Vision, Amnesty International, Jesuit Refugee Services, Save the Children, Care, Concern, USAID, Military experts from the U.S., U.K., Canada, Australia, and Pakistan. The United Nations contributors include two Secretary Generals as well as the Directors of the High Commission for Refugees, UNWRA, DHA, OCHA, UNDP, UNICEF, DPKO, et. al. All royalties from this *International Humanitarian Affairs Book Series* go toward the training of humanitarian workers.

I concluded several books with a poem; this is the first stanza from one by Sir Francis Drake in the 16th Century and should encourage those of us privileged to play a role in international humanitarian

assistance to be courageous in our noble
efforts:

"Disturb us, Lord, when
We are too well pleased with ourselves,
When our dreams have come true
Because we have dreamed too little,
When we arrived safely
Because we sailed too close to the shore."

Breaking Barriers

A golden thread in an antique tapestry provides strength to the fabric, continuity to the design and, if you are creative and open to innovation, a new image can emerge by combining different elements—by breaking traditional barriers that all too often constrain our vision.

For over a half century I have explored the links between medicine, diplomacy and humanitarian assistance, and suggest that some of these experiences are relevant to the challenges posed by the current pandemic.

Like so many activities in our lives this one began almost by accident. Medicine is not a pure science; especially in the chaos of an epidemic there are many cultural, philosophic and moral forces that must be considered. Identifying the causative agent of an infection, or even providing the correct drug regimen, are but part of a proper public health response, and that is where the art of medicine comes into play. Furthermore actions take place in an historical setting. The United States in the mid to late 1960s was a time of great tension over our war in Vietnam.

My interest at that time in diplomacy was part of an effort to present a peaceful alternative to the purely militaristic approach of the American government. My writings became the basis for Congressional Hearings in both the House of Representatives and the Senate. A Bill (HR10042) was drafted—and defeated—when the Nixon Administration saw it as an attack on their foreign policy, which it clearly was. But while the Bill failed, the ideas did not die, and I authored numerous articles and books, organized academic and United Nations symposia on these themes in which the methodology of public health, and even the semantics of medicine, were applied to the nuanced dialogue of diplomacy. The approach became a focus for senior figures in foreign policy. Slowly, over many decades, the early concepts became more organized into a formal program.

Cyrus Vance, a former U.S. Secretary of State, wrote about his late conversion to the central importance of health and humanitarian assistance in foreign affairs. Boutros Boutros Ghali, the former Secretary-General of the United Nations, when asked what he thought would be his most important legacy responded: "My work with Dr. Cahill in the mid-1990s on Preventive Diplomacy" (mentioned in *Milestones in Humanitarian Action)*. I recently had the pleasure of opening a new Center with this focus in Cairo, Egypt and in Brussels, there is another such Institute sponsored by France, Canada and Belgium.

Tenacity is a virtue that one learned in previous epidemics and has great value as we deal with the myriad, but not unprecedented, demands of the current pandemic, whether one is serving on the frontline in a hospital or government position, or offering reflections in the isolation of quarantine. I receive numerous calls from around the world every day seeking counsel and advice based on a lifetime of service in earlier epidemics.

Today is my birthday; celebrated, when I was a child, with parents and siblings giving home-made gifts—a poem, song or drawing, or cupcakes. With that spirit of joy and solidarity I share this message with our global CIHC/IIHA family and hope you remain safe, serving your fellow brothers and sisters.

Art and Artifacts

Many of the CIHC/IIHA Directors, faculty, tutors, and students, have visited my medical office in New York and a Long Island beach home where I do most of my writing in a library overlooking the Atlantic ocean. Today's report is stimulated by some of the artifacts that were brought back from humanitarian relief operations around the world; they were mostly gifts from local colleagues, or government officials. Almost all were items reflecting the cultures of the area. While few have financial value, they were an essential part of those experiences, and are the bases for long-term memories of journeys, a visual equivalent to a written diary.

Now, still in the isolation of quarantine, and in a silence only broken by the sound of the ocean waves and the song of birds, I share with you some description of my art and artifact collection, probably knowing each of you could match these with your own fascinating mementoes and tales. I have always loved artistic expression, but do not have the easy command of that vocabulary to succinctly state my observations.

There is a current traveling exhibit based on my 36 journeys to Somalia, some after droughts, floods or conflicts, and some for epidemiologic research. When I first went to Somalia in the early 1960s there was no written language. Somalia's culture is primarily an oral one. Traditions were passed through generations by poems and stories. I was accepted because of my medical service, a bridge into a closed society. Somalia is a barren, semi-desert land without the hard woods or metals that could be crafted into Central and West African art. In lower Somalia there are riverine areas but the trees are sparse and soft. Therefore, most artifacts in the exhibition are products intended for local, daily use rather than pieces created for museums.

One of my favorite pieces is a crude wooden camel milk bucket. Part of my research was obtaining numerous blood samples for later analysis in the United States of America. After explaining to the Somali Elders, sitting in the shade of a thorn tree, agreement would be formalized by sharing a bowl of camel's milk, enriched with blood from the animal's jugular vein. Even with dirt and insects floating to the top one knew that not to drink would be insulting, and probably end their endorsement. So I drank the concoction, sometimes without any bad effects.

Another item in the exhibit is a pair of crude—but comfortable—sandals made for me from camel skin by an artisan in the early 1960s. With extensive repairs over the decades, these became my footwear in trekking the full length of Somalia with the nomads. It took over three years, in interrupted journeys, through bush, desert, and riverine areas from the Ogaden desert and Hargeisa in the North to Kismayo at the southern point of the country.

Another item from those journeys is a carved headrest that allowed the proud tribesmen to keep their heads clear of the dust and dirt and ground-dwelling insects. It worked for me as well. Other local products brought back to New York include: (a) a fly whisk—an essential tool on the Horn, (b) typical cow bells, (c) an antique woven cloth bag and food mat, (d) a woven basket covered with cowrie shells, (e) woven baskets for dried meat, (f) a coastal wood carving from an old door frame, (g) a camel tooth necklace, (h) bridal gifts—amber, agate and other stones, and they all continue to enrich my life.

There were many other areas where I also worked or carried on research. For example, deep in the Western Desert of Egypt the

Siwa Oasis has for many centuries provided water and dates for nomads and a basic agricultural community. Alexander the Great visited Siwa in 332 BC, and various cultures left their imprints. I gathered shards of pottery in the surrounding dunes with images of chalices and other symbols of Christianity, documenting an almost forgotten phase in the life of that isolated oasis.

From Yemen I was given a number of traditional daggers (Jambiya) as a measure of the solidarity one builds after multiple trips in that long tortured land. An interesting feature of some Yemeni jewelry is that the best pieces were crafted by a small group of Jewish artisans; this skill was passed from father to son over many generations. One can find a Star of David in many Yemeni silver bracelets or necklaces. When Tariq Aziz, the former Deputy Prime Minister and Foreign Minister of Iraq under Saddam Hussein wanted to thank me for medical assistance he gave me three needle point panels from his family home. He told me that when their government was overthrown, which he fully expected, he wanted these preserved by someone who would appreciate their significance in his life.

Appreciating art and artifacts, even in the midst of humanitarian crises, is not without its disappointments. As I look around my library, with Amharic healing scrolls and manuscripts from the highlands of Ethiopia and Arabic calligraphy and early Korans, I can recall self-inflicted failures. For example, a Prime Minister of Sudan once wanted to present me with the original Koran of the Mahdi. I rejected his gift saying that it should remain in his country as part of their national patrimony. With a prescience I did not have, he stated "someday I will be overthrown and they will loot my home including my library and all will be lost." He was correct in his prediction, and I should have accepted his deeply personal gift. I foolishly judged a world he knew far better than I for much was ultimately destroyed in another folly of political hatred.

A similar fate awaited a personal collection of early Korans in Mogadishu that was part of a lifetime dream of an Italian colonialist to donate a library to Somalia. But it was a time of turmoil in Somalia and most Italians were fleeing. He wished me to accept his books and manuscripts and take them to safety in America. I once again, wrongly, thought it best to preserve them there. I accepted a single gift and it survived, but within a few years, all the rest was destroyed, and I bear a burden of guilt about my somewhat arrogant decision not to preserve an amateur collector's treasured library.

In Nicaraguan culture, images of angels are prominent and there are crocheted examples as well as carved statuettes in my office. There are also Dinka spears and crocodile shields from the Sudan, both gifts for delivering a baby, or for other medical services. We lived in Cairo Egypt in the early 1960s, and that was a period where many unusual artifacts were available. The Royal homes of King Farouk—and his family—were being abandoned; the large community of English and French expatriates had been ejected after the Suez crisis, and their homes and contents were being disposed at a fraction of their value. As an important element in this story, the U.S. Navy would be shipping our household goods to America. That combination of good fortunes allowed us to obtain some larger items such as antique doors, carved tombstones, segments of mosaic arches, Mashrabiya screens, and desks, chairs and beds with inlaid mother of pearl. These eventually were recreated into our Islamic apartment in New York, one so unusual that the Metropolitan Museum of Art has held meetings there for curators, scholars and potential donors.

From Dublin, having served as Professor and Chairman of the Department of Tropical Medicine at the Royal College of Surgeons in Ireland for 36 years (and taught over 4,000 medical students from all over Europe), I met many individuals outside of the medical community and was able to gradually build a nice collection of contemporary paintings—mostly gifts from the artists.

The above notes may seem to describe only isolated pieces, but the collection offers, at least to me, evidence of a unique coherence where art is an integral part of our being. For international humanitarian workers who have had the privilege of intimate contact with indigenous cultures, the gifts received from around the world after service in times of crisis are the basis for lasting memories. They are also tools to educate visitors in your homes or offices of the universal wonder of the visual expressions of beauty. I hope you have had the same joy from forming a collection similar to this tale, and that some memories of this pandemic period will be a part of them.

The Drain Works

During the past few months of enforced isolation I have written a series of brief essays to our thousands of alumni in humanitarian relief and tropical medicine working all around the world in different capacities. The purpose of those 'Perspectives' was to review lessons learned from previous epidemics, and to foster a sense of "family" as we, each in our own way, deal with the current COVID-19 pandemic. For the next phase in these reflections there will be a focus on advice offered by mentors that influenced, beyond their immediate intention, my approach to life.

Alan Woodruff, M.D., Ph.D. was my Professor at the London School and Hospital for Tropical Diseases in the early 1960s. I spent a wonderful year in daily contact with him—learning in the classroom, laboratory and, particularly at the bedside, of sick patients how to diagnose and treat a wide range of parasitic and infectious diseases, and to develop research protocols for advanced study.

He had many interests beyond medicine— he was a gifted woodblock artist, a lover of music, and a generous host. After I left for the Middle East and Africa he, as a good Professor, stayed in regular contact and wrote a very generous Foreword to my first textbook. When he retired from the London School, at that time the most prestigious academic position in our field, he accepted a much more modest assignment to establish a new medical school in Juba, South Sudan.

A few years later I asked him what he thought his greatest accomplishment there had been. With a humility I have never forgotten, he paused and said, "I think the drain in the front of the clinic is working". Progress can be very slow indeed in the tropics. Another unmistakable lesson in that answer was that no task should be seen as beneath our personal concern. If clearing the water and mud allows access to the clinic then that removes an important obstacle in the healing process. It also reminds us that humility is a great virtue.

His philosophy seems still relevant to our struggles in the confusion and change in our current COVID-19 pandemic world. In honor of Professor Woodruff the attached extract from an early article of mine is enclosed. The wisdom he transmitted to this grateful student enabled me to never lose sight of the details, even in the midst of a global tragedy.

Beirut's Smell of Death (NY Times, 1982)
Armenian Scholars no longer search for
God in the Near East School of Theology
in West Beirut. The cool archives room in
the cellar is now a blood bank, and the
conference hall where ecclesiastical nu-
ances were once the topic of discussion
now contains two operating tables for as-
sembly line amputations and a bin for
severed limbs.
Statistics are a game that politicians play
in war. People far from the scene are
having a great debate in the American
press about the accuracy of death figures
in Lebanon. But there is nothing subtle
about the current carnage in Beirut if
one can recognize blood, or smell a fes-
tering wound, or feel the feverish head of
a dying child. There is no mystery about
the scope of this tragedy, if one walks
the wards of the hospital in the School
of Theology and sees the limbless bodies,
the fractured faces, the blind, the burned.
These are real people, men and women
and children, hundreds of them, and no
amount of sophistry can dehumanize the
horrors of this war into a sterile column
of figures. They were not numbers I ex-
amined; they were the innocent civilian

debris of a war not of their making but caused by policies that have left them a stateless people. Now they have their dead and their maimed to nourish their hatred and determination.

Unless the indiscriminate bombing and shelling cease for good, the load of shattered limbs discarded from the Near East School of Theology will grow. While the wise men struggle slowly with the semantics of peace, panic-stricken victims scream psychotically in halls where scholars once pondered the words of God. Hatred abounds, and the legacy of bitterness that will be reflected a generation hence in cripples on the streets of Beirut will pose a greater threat to the security of the area than militaristic minds seem capable of considering now.

The painful process toward reconciliation and eventual peace may be best symbolized today in the joint efforts at healing by Armenians, Palestinians, Christian, Muslim Lebanese, Norwegian volunteers, and this American who shall long remember the privilege of making clinical rounds in a School of Theology. Examining patients while shells exploded and fires raged nearby, and with the sick smell of death and disease overwhelming my senses, I wondered what ends could ever justify these means.

An Unexpected Help

The AIDS epidemic began more slowly than the current COVID-19 pandemic. Before a clear clinical pattern emerged, physicians dealing primarily with parasitic and infectious diseases diagnosed isolated cases of patients with puzzling immune deficiencies, and an almost always fatal outcome.

I began to see AIDS patients in 1979 and, by 1982, almost all had died within a year. At the time we had not identified the cause, and could only treat secondary complications. We made mistakes in categorizing vulnerable groups; for example, at one point we thought there was a special predilection in the Haitian community, and in another error we overly prescribed chemotherapy for one of the cancer manifestations (*Kaposi's sarcoma*), thereby further depressing those patients' immune systems. As the number of cases increased it became obvious that this was a contagious outbreak, and that direct contact was important. It was also evident that blood, and other bodily fluids, had a significant role in transmission with persons receiving regular transfusions (e.g. hemophiliacs) often affected.

In the early days of the AIDS epidemic there were many similarities to our response to the COVID-19 pandemic. There was fear on the part of health workers as to how to protect themselves and their families while providing care, there was a lack of essential data, confusion in terminology, episodes of denial, and unwarranted blame attributed in the chain of political responsibility. There was a shameful silence from governmental agencies and from much of the medical and research establishment, a silence clearly due to the fact that many of the victims were then considered on the fringes of society—homosexuals, drug addicts, and prostitutes.

Because parasitic infections were a primary cause of death I treated a very large number of early AIDS patients, and I sought, with some colleagues from the U.S. CDC, the support of the Federal government. Our efforts were not very successful. Senator Edward Kennedy was sympathetic to our appeal, but suggested that a basic first step was needed to identify leading authorities from across the country to contribute to a book that he could present to officials in Washington, DC.

This 'Perspective' tells a remarkable story of the impact that a single person had in changing our national attitude to AIDS, and may be relevant to our search for global leadership in the current pandemic.

Terence Cardinal Cooke, the Catholic Archbishop of New York, was seriously ill in the spring of 1983, and required frequent home visits. Shortly before our planned AIDS Symposium he asked me, "How is it going?", and I answered not very well, explaining that many political decision-makers had not responded to our invitation. He asked what he could do to help and—with only a two-day notice—offered to attend the conference and deliver an Invocation. Once it was known that Cardinal Cooke would open our program we received urgent calls from the Mayor's office and from local Congressmen that also wished to participate, an attitude that had been sadly absent till then.

Enclosed is the text of Cardinal Cooke's comments:

Mister Mayor, Dr. Cahill, my friends of the medical community I salute each of you as we come together from all over the United States on this Sunday in spring here at Lenox Hill Hospital in New York City.

You represent many different professions within the health care community. I understand there are here today doctors, nurses, scientists, researchers, technicians and technologists, and many other dedicated people. You have assembled because of your concern about a major epidemic in our country that is affecting an ever-growing number of people and that has resulted already in the loss of so many lives. I support you in your daily, courageous efforts in facing this danger and in meeting this challenge.

You are here also because you are convinced that individually and collectively you have God-given powers to strengthen your brothers and sisters and to heal them. You know from experience that in teamwork and cooperation there is solid hope in finding answers to perplexing questions. This spirit of teamwork must go beyond the medical community and involve people of religious, private and governmental sectors in making sure that this crisis becomes an opportunity to serve. In areas of research especially, in the pooling of information and knowledge, we can penetrate unknown boundaries and arrive at solutions to human problems which only seem insoluble.

You are here above all else because you are loving, caring people. Each person's pain is pain to you; each person's joy is your own. You understand the elements of the AIDS epidemic in terms of the pain and the anxiety and the fear of the individual human being—the patient—who is suffering. And you will use your skills and the scientific data which you share today to help that person.

I am one with you in your concern, and I Rejoice that you are people of hope. We represent many different faiths and philosophies of life. I invite you to pray with me as we begin this important day.

Heavenly Father, eternal spirit of wisdom and healing, we acknowledge your presence among us, and we thank you for the powers which you have given us, especially the power of healing.

Lord, we pray for our brothers and sisters who are suffering from the Acquired Immune Deficiency Syndrome, and for their families and friends. We ask you to inspire the members of the medical profession who are striving to strengthen and support and heal them.

Lord, as we face this crisis together, make

*us instruments of your peace. Heal our di-
visions and deepen our Unity. Renew our
hope, and bring a sense of joy into our
lives and the lives of those we serve.*

*Lord, replace the anxiety within us with
a quiet confidence. Replace the tension
within us with a holy relaxation. Replace
the turbulence within us with a sacred
calm. Replace the coldness within us with
a loving warmth.*

*Father, we are united in this prayer and
in a spirit of faith, of Hope, and of love.
We ask you to assist and bless us always
get our work to help our brothers and sisters in your one human family. Amen.*

As we listened to the Cardinal's passionate
identification with those suffering from
AIDS, and the healthcare workers treating
them, we knew we were witnessing history in the making. There was still a long
road ahead, and many obstacles to be over-
come in the struggle to make AIDS a major
focus of medical and public health attention in the United States, but a critical step
was taken on that spring day in 1983, with
one man's courage and clarion call. Without Cardinal Cooke's intercession we were
voices without an audience. The resulting

book—*The AIDS Epidemic*—was circulated within government and medical circles in the United States; and widely translated for the European and Asian market.

Cardinal Cooke died only a few months later. Especially—in these difficult times—the quiet yet iron strength of this remarkable mentor is a constant reminder for always speaking out for truth and justice.

Hopefully you—as humanitarian aid workers, and as individuals—can involve some unexpected hero to bring wise, and essential, attention to the pandemic and other crises that currently face us.

Focus on the Individual

At the start of an enforced isolation due to the global spread of the lethal COVID-19 virus I began a series of weekly essays for our humanitarian alumni to maintain unity as each, in our own ways, tried to deal with the challenges of a pandemic.

Were there lessons from earlier epidemics that might prove helpful? Were there virtues, and related disciplines, in the struggle? Could one cite individual acts of wisdom, or heroism, that offered examples from the past for the present? These 'Perspectives' served their purpose, if judged by the many responses. I close this initial phase with a short eulogy offered to a remarkable woman who always helped keep a personal focus on our efforts. She never allowed me to forget the individual in the chaos of disaster, and to maintain that emphasis in our academic courses, and in the International Humanitarian Affairs Book Series in training programs of the United Nations, national and international agencies and non-governmental organizations (NGOs) around the world.

Joan Durkin worked with me for 41 years. She was hired after we spoke over the telephone but before we had met in person. It was a particularly busy time in my medical office with the front consulting room being used daily by a Congressman plotting with the former Mayor of New York City a campaign for the position of Governor of New York State. Joan was a receptionist at a Catholic rectory but could not hold a regular job because she was not a U.S. citizen and did not hold a Green Card.

In those years immigration was not a significant issue and certain positions and countries (medical secretary and Ireland) were favored. I went into my front room and said to the ex-Mayor and the Congressman-candidate "there is a woman on the phone I would like to hire, and she needs a Green Card; either get her the permit or get out of my office." She received her Green Card the following day, and began working in the office that afternoon. I don't think she ever missed a day, or was even late, till she suddenly died of a cerebral hemorrhage 41 years later. The eulogy I gave at her funeral is provided here:

When the Durkin family asked that I speak today, my thoughts went back to my first meeting with this remarkable woman. At the time I did not see her warm smile or red hair, for my introduction was to her voice on a telephone, that confident solid lilt with a soft Sligo accent. Somehow, I knew that I had discovered something wonderful. I asked if she would work with me, and she started the next day. My sense of wonder and gratitude at that decision grew stronger over the next 41 years, and it only ended, in a way, when she died.

Joan never worked for me; she worked with me. She was my partner, and put her unique stamp on all we did together. Our so-called work embraced a very complex, almost magical, world. Yes, we cared for the sick, the lonely, the vulnerable, the elderly, and we shared in the joys of healing and recovery. Joan never lost sight of her essential role, and she made certain that it remained mine, and that was always to focus on the individual. I could indulge in grand plans to change the world but she would, gently but firmly, bring me back to earth, always to the individual. She was the caring, compassionate public face of a medical practice that served, among others, thousands of missionaries and our global community of humanitarian relief workers. And she knew them all by name.

In the early days of the AIDS epidemic,

when everyone died too soon, some of our patients would say to me, hoping against hope, that "her soup may be better than your medicine." Joan would finish her usual long day at the office, and then see nothing unusual about traveling around the city to our patients, bringing meals, and her special nourishment, to frightened souls.

With our United Nations patients, this woman from rural Ireland somehow had the inbred sensitivity, and unique capacity, to make people from different cultures and traditions feel comfortable in that strange and confusing time of illness, when fears can be overwhelming, and confidence has to be restored to allow essential decisions.

Today I think it not inappropriate for the Cahills to claim her as a member of our clan. I am certain there are many others in this church, and many, many others who could not be with us, who feel that bond. In the last few days alone, scores—maybe hundreds—called referring to her as "our Joan", feeling that they were part of her, and that she was an integral part of their lives. One final reflection on her personality which I knew, admired and loved on a daily basis for over four decades was she had the rare gift to subtly, but very effectively, deflect any attempt to praise her; she would change the topic of gratitude by laughter or gentle cynicism. Today we thank her for being "Joan".

A brilliant light has gone out of this world; an irretrievable one for me and for many. But we would not honor Joan if we did not move ahead with strength and courage. As one of her favorite poets, WB Yeats, phrased it, "we are bred to a harder thing than triumph". So, let us go forth together, aware of the great privilege we have had to share in her life. May her beautiful soul rest in peace.

The pause in these 'Perspectives' reflects the demands of re-opening a medical office with new regulations regarding safe distancing, masks, gowns and gloves. But this essay takes us back to the original goals of the series—to review our own experiences, and face the unknown as a family of humanitarian workers devoted to the less fortunate, those in need, and to proceed with joy and confidence. Do stay in touch with Brendan, and I shall write to you all again soon.

About the CIHC

The copyright for this book has been transferred to the Center for International Humanitarian Cooperation (CIHC) and allows royalties to go directly towards the training of humanitarian workers. The CIHC is a U.S. Registered Public Charity that was founded in 1992 to promote healing and peace in countries shattered by natural disasters, armed conflicts, and ethnic violence. The CIHC employs its resources and unique personal contacts to stimulate interest in humanitarian issues and to promote innovative educational programs and training models. Our extensive list of publications and regular symposia address both the basic issues, and the emerging challenges, of international humanitarian assistance.

Since 2001, the CIHC has supported training in humanitarian activities, most notably the Institute of International Humanitarian Affairs (IIHA) at Fordham University. We have graduated over 3,000 relief workers from 140 nations, and continue to offer programs in Europe, Asia, Africa, Latin America and North America. The IIHA also offers Master Degrees as well as an undergraduate Major in humanitarian affairs. The CIHC has formal partnerships with the

Royal College of Surgeons in Ireland, University College Dublin, the NOHA network of European universities, United Nations World Food Programme (WFP), International Organization of Migration (IOM), International Medical Corps (IMC), Action Contre la Faim (ACF), Jesuit Refugee Service (JRS), the British Ministry of Defense, and other UN, NGO and governmental organizations.

Support the CIHC

With your donation we provide courses, trainings, and symposia, offering dozens of scholarships to students from the Global South, and conducting ongoing research and publications to promote best practices in humanitarian affairs. Please consider a recurring gift.

Donate online through our secure payment processor at:
www.cihc.org/support

You can also mail your gift to CIHC at:
850 Fifth Avenue, New York, NY 10065

We also accept donations of airlines miles, investments, bequests, etc.
Please contact us at:
mail@cihc.org
or *(212)-636-6294* to discuss.

About the Refuge Press

This book, published by *The Refuge Press,* continues the International Humanitarian Affairs (IHA) Book Series and is distributed by Fordham University Press.The IHA Book Series has published seventeen volumes on various aspects of providing relief in complex humanitarian crises. The IHA texts are widely used in universities and training programs around the world and have been translated into numerous languages. They are available in print and digital form. *Occasional Papers* complement the books on specific historical topics.

Lightning Source UK Ltd.
Milton Keynes UK
UKHW010703061022
410025UK00008B/322